# THE GRAND BANKS

by Bern Keating

Photographs by Dan Guravich

Rand McNally & Company

*Chicago* • *New York* • *San Francisco*

Other Books by Bern Keating

*THE HORSE THAT WON THE CIVIL WAR*

*INVADERS OF ROME*

*LIFE AND DEATH OF THE AZTEC NATION*

*MOSQUITO FLEET*

*ZEBULON PIKE*

*CHAKA, KING OF THE ZULUS*

To Pau Pau, sweet
friend and beloved
daughter

# Newfoundland

0     100     200
Miles

C. CHIDLEY

N. AULATSIVIK I.

CIRQUE MTN. 5,160 FT.
(HIGHEST POINT IN NEWFOUNDLAND)

Saglek Bay

Hebron

*TORNGAT MTS.*

*KAUMAJET MTS.*

*LABRADOR*

SOUTH AULATSIVIK I.

Nain

*Koraluk R.*

Mistastin L.

Hopedale

Scheffeville
(Knob Lake)

*Attikamagen L.*

*HIGHLAND*

C. HARRISON

*Dyke L.*

*Naskaupi R.*

*Kaipokok River*

Hamilton Inlet

Menihek Lakes

*Sandgirt L.*

*Lobstick L.*

*Michikamau L.*

Sandwich Bay

Shabogamo L.

*Ossokmanuan L.*

*Churchill River*

Happy Valley

Lake Melville

*MEALY MTS.*

Wabush L.

*Eagle River*

Alexis R.

St. Michaels Bay

*Lac Joseph*

*Atikonak L.*

Ashuanipi L.

*Little Mecatina R.*

BRADORE HILLS

BELLE ISLE

*Strait of Belle Isle*

Hare Bay

GREY IS.

*LONG RANGE MTS.*

*White Bay*

C. ST. JOHN

*Notre Dame Bay*

FOGO I.

C. FREELS

*Bonavista Bay*

Corner Brook

Gander

C. BONAVISTA

C. ST. GEORGE

*Grand L.*

*Exploits R.*

TERRA NOVA NAT'L PARK

*Trinity Bay*

*St. George's Bay*

*LONG RANGE MTS.*

*Meelpaeg L.*

MT. SYLVESTER 1,250 FT.

Harbour Grace

Conception Bay

C. RAY

Port-aux-Basques

*Fortune Bay*

Marystown

**ST. JOHN'S**

AVALON PENINSULA

MIQUELON

BURIN PEN.

Trepassey

LANGLADE

*Placentia Bay*

ST. PIERRE

*St. Mary's Bay*

C. RACE

Shotts

*The surface of Newfoundland is rough, carved by glaciers of long ago. Rough, too, are its surrounding seas. And on its vast and fertile fishing ground, the Grand Banks, churned by the clash of icy and warm currents, ride dense fogs and icebergs—constant hazards for the fishermen of many nations.*

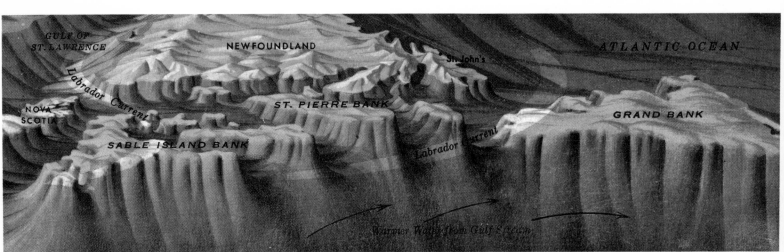

GULF OF ST. LAWRENCE

NEWFOUNDLAND

ATLANTIC OCEAN

*Labrador Current*

St. John's

NOVA SCOTIA

ST. PIERRE BANK

GRAND BANK

SABLE ISLAND BANK

*Labrador Current*

*Warmer Water from Gulf Stream*

# Prefatory Note

Many writers on the Northwest Atlantic fisheries are confused in their geographic terminology about the Newfoundland fisheries. In this book I have followed the traditional practice of differentiating between the Newfoundland Banks and the Grand Bank, which is only one of the Newfoundland Banks, though by far the largest and richest. Others include Green Bank, St. Pierre Bank, Burgeo Bank, and Flemish Cap.

# Contents

# 1

# The Pyramid of Life

*...where the Northern Ocean in vast whirls*
*Boils round the naked melancholy isles...*

Over the Grand Bank the trawler heaved and plunged under the last of the freezing winter gales. Sailors knocked ice from the rigging with mallets to keep the ship from capsizing under its weight. Spray froze on my pea jacket, and the wind cut through my clothing like an ice pick. So I spent long hours out of the weather, chatting with off-duty sailors thawing out in the galley. Seas crashed against our bow. The trawler shuddered and slid down the wave's far slope.

For a week I huddled inside and cozily watched the bread dough rise in the galley's warmth.

One morning the wind abated and I climbed to the wheelhouse. The stormy eastern gale was shifting to the south.

"Breeze comin' from duh suddard," the skipper said. "Always blows up mauzy weather."

And a fog did indeed roll over the deep as the warm south wind hit the chill air of the bank. It veiled the face of the sun but brought the first soft hint of spring.

Ashore that southern breeze blew across the rocky outcroppings and frozen lakes of Newfoundland, loosening the grip of winter's ice. Snow fell from spruce branches and plopped into gushing torrents. Moose and caribou felt the strange wanderlust that returns to them with the season. Fishermen in the outports spread their nets and made their wooden needles fly, repairing last summer's ravages to prepare for the spawning visit of sea creatures to the shallow waters about the island.

But spring came reluctantly on land, its pace measured by the agonizingly slow retreat of snowbank and ice sheet. Not so at sea.

As it has for countless ages, in the next few days the sea's surface responded to the first warmth with an explosion of proliferating life. Too small for us to see except as a faint blush of color on the waves, countless trillions of phytoplankton, sea plants so tiny a dozen million inhabit every gallon of water over the banks, roused themselves from winter dormancy and began to split their single-celled bodies in two, doubling every two or three days during the peak of the spring bloom. Somehow the microscopic plants regain their marvelous shapes after the split, becoming again — according to their species — drums, golf balls and tees, bracelets, needles, fishhooks, anchors. Drifting with the southern wind, the plants basked in the fog-filtered sunlight, working the miracle of converting the distant sun's energy to living tissue, turning mineral from the sea into vegetable, the stuff of all life, the base of the vast pyramid of sea creatures that ultimately feed directly or indirectly on those teeming sea pastures. Because the sun's rays quickly fade as they penetrate even the clearest water, few sea plants flourish below 600 feet and most pass their short lives in shallows of less than 100 feet, so the springtime drama is played close to the surface where the seafarer can witness it.

With the plants drifted a host of creatures which graze those surface meadows. Clouds of shrimplike copepods, most of them no larger than a pinhead, fed on the teeming sea plants. The larvae and young of thousands of species devoured the phytoplankton; crabs, lobsters, herring, mackerel, even the bottom-dwelling flatfish send their young aloft in spring to fatten at the surface before sinking again forever to the ocean floor. Among that swarm of drifters riding the ocean currents floated minuscule but savage predators.

Hated by fishermen for stealing the fish's food, comb jellies snared the copepods and the larvae of herring with sticky tentacles which they reeled in for all the world like spinning tackle. Arrowworms darted after copepods with appalling ferocity.

The trawler plowed through immense carpets of jellyfish, uncountable millions of the undulating transparent umbrellas, their tentacles mindlessly probing for hapless creatures that drifted within reach of their lethal stingers. Although they lack even a rudimentary brain, the jellyfish have worked out an arrangement with the haddock. We saw tiny schools of young fish hovering for protection under the stinging tentacles in exchange for acting as bait to lure larger fish within range.

These carnivores can move fast enough to chase down their prey, but they cannot propel themselves farther than the death pounce, and they, like that seemingly endless carpet of jelly-fish, must helplessly ride the currents with the sea plants.

Through the swarms of drifters, plant and animal, plowed great schools of fish, first creatures of sea life capable of traveling where they will to find their prey. In uncountable billions herring, capelin, and launce gorged themselves on the springtime feast.

In the trawler's wheelhouse, the Fathometer picked up a school of herring packed so solidly that its echo traces on the drum showed as black as the bottom itself. The skipper crossed the school, measured it at two miles wide, then turned to run the length of it. For hours we churned along over that one school and the echo trace held steady. The numbers contained within that incredible river of fish lie beyond human imagining.

Out of the fog loomed a pod of baleen whales. Swimming across the banks with mouths agape, they strained torrents of seawater through sievelike whalebone curtains in their mouths and licked off the harvest of creatures too coarse to pass the strainer. Daily the blue whale, largest animal that ever inhabited the earth, much larger than the greatest of the dinosaurs, must consume two tons of the near-microscopic drifters to maintain its enormous bulk.

A single humpback whale slashed across our school of herring. That humpback must have a daily ration of 5,000 herring. Each herring eats 7,000 copepods, and each copepod devours 130,000 phytoplankton a day to stay alive. So it took 4½ trillion of the sea plants created that day to support this one whale.

And still the drifters multiplied faster than they were devoured.

Around the flanks of the schools of fish, like wolves harassing herds of caribou, swam the large predatory fish — insatiable tuna that double in size to 400 pounds and more during a brief northward migration, porpoises that swam rings around our lumbering trawler with dazzling grace and speed, devouring the fish confused by our trawler's passage, and finback whales running down the 2,500 pounds of capelin they must eat every day.

Most ferocious of all were the codfish, bottom feeders that come to the top for the springtime gourmandising and will strike at virtually anything — animal, vegetable, or mineral. We passed a school of capelin fleeing the codfish and packed so tightly that a ridge of live wriggling fish rose above the water.

Around the trawler skimmed the seabirds come to join the feast. Kittiwakes, terns, razorbills, murres, gulls, and puffins wheeled and plunged into the icy waters. Through the fog we heard harsh cries of thousands of more distant birds, all the unlovely sounds — mewings, squawkings, skirlings — of the seafowl.

Elsewhere in the world's oceans, as the phytoplankton exhaust the sea's minerals the springtime growth slows and finally almost stops till the winds of autumn stir the waters and bring up a fresh supply of minerals from the deeps where they have settled during the summer. But on the Grand Bank the warm weather bloom persists, and the population of creatures living on the sea plants reaches stupendous numbers. Nowhere else does life explode with such fecundity as in the improbable cradle of the icy and fogbound waters of the Grand Bank.

To me, a landsman from the temperate south, the ice and fog seemed hostile to life, but they provide the clue to the bank's fertility.

Thousands of miles south, trade winds push warm tropical waters out of the Caribbean Sea, through the straits between Yucatan and Cuba and into the shallow Gulf of Mexico. The warm waters pile up in the gulf's basin, and the surface rises several inches higher than the sea outside. Pent-up gulf waters pour through the opening between Florida and Cuba and run downhill into the Atlantic, forming an immense river in the sea, a torrent 1,000 times greater than the Mississippi River. Every hour 14 cubic miles of warm gulf water pour into the Atlantic, often at four miles and more per hour. Prevailing winds and the earth's rotation push the river toward the northeast. When the stream reaches the seaward bulge of Cape Hatteras, on the North Carolina coast, and is shunted farther eastward, the surface temperature still hovers at about 88° F. in summer. Swirling snow of the coast's winter storms falls into water warm enough for a tepid bath. The stream carries a heavier freight of salt than the sea around it, and in its waters ride exotic creatures of the south — tropical shrimp, crabs, worms, sea plants.

Almost exactly the same distance northwest of the Grand Bank as the fountainhead of the warm Gulf Stream lies to the southwest, cold waters of the Arctic Ocean pour southward through the narrow straits between Greenland's ice cap and the perpetually frozen outpost islands of North America. The stream picks up frigid overflow waters from the straits and fjords of icy coasts on both sides of Baffin Bay.

Providentially, on the Grand Bank where the two mighty rivers collide, the floor of the sea has thrust upward and formed a plateau 350 miles long, 200 miles wide, and almost everywhere so shallow that the sun's rays penetrate to the very ocean floor with enough force to nurse a lusty bloom of phytoplankton.

On this Grand Bank, as the plants consume the sea's vital minerals, however, they do not exhaust the stock, for the gray-green Arctic Current and the blue Gulf Stream come together with a mighty churning of waters. Warm breezes from the south hit the Arctic breath of the northern current and dump their load of moisture as a fog which thins and thickens with the shifting of the winds but in spring and early summer rarely disappears entirely. Warm salty waters of the tropics hit chill brackish waters of the Arctic and spin off darting currents, eddies, swirls which churn up the lowest layers along the floor of the banks. The phosphates and nitrates vital to sustaining the plankton bloom swirl up from the floor, where they tend to settle, and mix again with surface waters. Ice floating on the Arctic stream melts and drops mineral debris picked up in the north as the parent glacier scraped across the land. Icebergs as big as skyscrapers melt and split, toppling their huge bulk and setting up more eddies on the bottom.

So turbulent are the shallow waters that during bad weather even the bottom-feeding codfish become seasick, vomit, and lose weight, leaving them famished and easily caught when the storm subsides.

The sides of the Grand Bank plateau slope sharply down into the abyss, the dark ocean deeps where plant life cannot exist, where a vast store of minerals carried by all the world's rivers has gathered untouched. Sucked up by the swirling eddies on the bank, great underwater currents rush up the slope from the abyss, carrying yet more minerals into the shallows.

Just north of the teeming shallows the plateau thrusts above the waves to form the triangular patch of rocky island called Newfoundland. Twice the island has been submerged as a proper part of the underwater plateau, once since the era of man; but it is rising now, and some channels in the fjords along the deeply indented coast are shoaling. Fishermen grumble that they are forever lengthening their wharves to reach the receding water. Twice glaciers have scraped across the land, scouring it free of most of the topsoil. Like the ridges on the sea bottom, almost all the island's bays, its hundreds of lakes and "ponds," and the rivers and ridges run southwest to northeast. Stunted birch, spruce, fir, and larch forest half the island. The rest is a boggy barren with a brief harvest of a dozen kinds of berries. Caribou, bear, fox, hares, and beaver have always lived there. Although a newcomer, the moose flourishes, and mink, escaping from cages on mink ranches, are spreading across the island.

Caught between the permanent Iceland low-pressure cell to the east and transient low-pressure areas blowing in from the continent to the west, Newfoundland's waters are troubled by violent storms. When the winds die down, the sempiternal fog moves in again. During the winter, only the southern ports are ice free. In springtime great fields of cake ice and towering icebergs in fantastic shapes drift down the coasts toward the banks. As they melt, the icebergs wallow, capsize, split, and calve their own smaller icebergs with great bellows of birth pain. From the land, the crack and boom of grinding ice floes sounds like distant cannon fire. A diffused light the sailors call "ice blink" hovers over the sea.

Forbidding as the landscape and surrounding waters are, hundreds of thousands of persons live there, some ashore and many on trawlers come to the shallow sea to chase vast schools of fish that breed there. On the radarscope, I once counted nearly 50 vessels plowing and replowing the sea through the fog, weaving weird patterns with their crisscrossing wakes, and miraculously avoiding collision.

For almost 500 years, and maybe more, maybe indeed many more years, hungry Europe has sent its boldest seamen to brave the storms, the ice, and the fogs of the banks to harvest the sea. In the savage struggle for existence on the Grand Bank, man, at the peak of the pyramid living on the humble plankton, had become the greatest predator of all.

In the Age of Exploration, neither England nor her colonies (of which Newfoundland is sometimes called the first) had gold or silver mines. Nor did the Portuguese, Basques, Gascons, Bretons, or Normans, so they worked on the banks and sold their salt cod for gold and silver coinage made from the wealth of Spain's colonial mines.

During the 500 years that European and island sailors worked the banks, they suffered cruel hardships and survived by becoming perhaps the world's toughest and most skillful fishing navy.

But the banks are changing. Progress has come in the form

of the giant factory ship, a seagoing assembly line where the patience to stand over a machine for eight hours has more survival value than the hardihood to knock ice from a boat's rigging in a blizzard.

I went to the Newfoundland Banks and traveled over the island to see a rude way of life before the romance of it vanished forever.

# 2

# Man Comes
# to the Grand Bank

*They that go down to the sea in ships, that do business in great waters.*

One of the oldest cities north of Mexico, St. John's on Newfoundland has remarkably few historical buildings or monuments, for disastrous fires leveled the city in the nineteenth century and decades of hard times have not encouraged spending on fripperies. One new historical monument stands facing the provincial capitol, however, a statue of the Portuguese navigator Gaspar Cortereal. The statue pleases me, partly because of its naive and oddly endearing ugliness and partly because of a sly impudence.

The Portuguese government gave the awkward statue to Newfoundland in gratitude for hospitality shown Portuguese fishermen of the banks during their revictualing visits to the harbor. Besides standing as a perpetual token of friendship, however, the statue also diplomatically reminds Newfoundland that the donors consider the island and its fish-swarming waters a Portuguese and not a British discovery, which its present owners insist it is. For years during the early days of exploration the island was called Cortereal. And the Portuguese sea captain may, indeed, have been there before John Cabot, who just possibly never saw Newfoundland at all, though British historians say he landed there first on St. John's Day in 1497.

In either case, other Europeans had been there before the Portuguese or the British.

Icelandic sagas of journeys to lands west of Greenland have long persuaded many historians that Vikings visited the New World around the year 1000. In 1440, a half-century before Columbus sailed westward supposedly into the unknown, a map appeared in Switzerland carrying a legend about Norse exploration and clearly showing knowledge of a vast country west of Europe's farthest outpost in Greenland. This map was discovered in 1957. Publication in 1965 of *The Vinland Map and The Tartar Relation* effectively destroyed what little serious opposition remained to the story of Viking travel to the Western Hemisphere — except, of course, among die-hard Italian students who refuse to yield their compatriot Columbus' claim to first discovery. The legend that accompanies the Vinland Map of 1440 reads:

> *By God's will after a long voyage from the island of Greenland to the south toward the most distant remaining parts of the western ocean sea, sailing southward amidst the ice, the companions Bjarni and Leif Eiriksson discovered a new land, extremely fertile and even*

*having vines, the which island they named Vinland. Eric, legate of the Apostolic See and bishop of Greenland and the neighboring regions, arrived in this truly vast and very rich land in the name of Almighty God, in the last year of our most blessed father Paschal, remained a long time in both summer and winter, and later returned northeastward toward Greenland and then proceeded in most humble obedience to the will of his superiors.*

As startling to me as the proof of pre-Columbian trips to the New World and widespread knowledge of its existence is the report of a bishop's yearlong visit to a Christian colony there as late as 1117, the last year of Pope Paschal II's life. Untidy as human beings are, more than a century of colonization should have left some debris for archaeologists to explore, some hint of where the fabled Vinland lay. For years before the Vinland Map was rediscovered, amateur and professional vinlandologists had searched with little luck for relics to prove Viking presence in Virginia, Massachusetts, Rhode Island, Canada's Maritime Provinces, and even in distant Minnesota, a thousand miles inland on a landlocked sea. And by its natural location athwart a southwestward course from Greenland, the island of Newfoundland suggested itself as the Viking home.

But doubts remained about Newfoundland as Vinland. Repeated mention in the sagas of great fertility, fruiting vines, year-around grazing, light frosts, and days and nights of even length hardly applies to an island scoured bare of topsoil by glaciers and buried under snow and ice during long winter nights.

Then in 1961 the Norwegian explorer and author Helge Ingstad found the ruins of Viking structures at L'Anse-au-Meadow, on the extreme northern tip of Newfoundland, the part closest to the parent colony in Greenland. Foundations of the "great hall" repeat exactly the floor plan of a communal center Leif Ericson built himself in Greenland. The Vikings smelted iron ore; carbon dating of the smelter charcoal shows it was burned in 1060, plus or minus 70 years, giving a spread of time almost exactly right to include the exploratory voyages of the sagas and the sojourn of the Bishop of Greenland.

Vinland nevertheless probably lies elsewhere, for graves of Viking explorers in Greenland have yielded lumps of coal from beds in Rhode Island, and the Viking New World outpost described in the sagas had too mild a climate for modern Newfoundland; but the first Europeans on the island, Vinland or not, were almost certainly Vikings.

And yet maybe not. The Irish have long insisted that St. Brendan and a band of Irish monks fled westward before Viking raids on their home monasteries a century and a half before Leif's voyage. Those Irish monks supposedly landed in the New World and converted the savages.

And one of the Icelandic poems, the "Eirikssaga," reports capturing two *skraelings* (as the Vikings called the aborigines of the New World) who told of a land farther west where white-skinned dwellers paraded in white clothes, carried poles to which clothes were attached, and "yelled" in a mighty voice — a splendid description of chanting monks in religious procession seen through savage eyes. The *skraelings* even called the region "White Man's Land."

Reports persist that the Micmac Indians of the Canadian

mainland west of Newfoundland greeted their supposed European discoverers with a cross and that they blessed themselves with the sign of the cross in the Catholic fashion.

A Venetian ambassador, writing home to describe 50 of the savages of Newfoundland kidnapped by Cortereal and exhibited to the Portuguese court, called them "white somewhat darkened by the cold." He noted that a few had green eyes and that the men were taller than Europeans. Later historians wrote that an occasional male of Newfoundland's Beothuk Indians stood well over six feet and had yellow hair. All the Beothuks wore their long hair in a Viking braid.

An Icelandic historian now living in Canada insists that the *skraelings* of the sagas were a vanished dark-skinned pygmy people who crossbred with Vikings to produce modern Canadian Eskimos. Eskimo mythology does talk of the *tunnits,* a tribe of tall blond conquerors, though with no sense of kinship. Much as historical legends and speculations fascinate adventurous scholars with the exciting possibility of being proved true, most historians find it hard to discover the Scandinavian ancestor hiding behind the Eskimo's flat nose, slit eyes, and bulging cheeks. So the Icelander's theory has attracted only one prominent disciple.

Even if the Icelander were right, a corporal's guard of nomadic Eskimos and the occasional blond Indian of a tribe long since extinct are all the Vikings left behind on Newfoundland, for they vanished sometime after the Greenland bishop's visit.

Many historians of Europe's maritime nations prowl dusty archives searching for proof that their compatriots crossed the Atlantic first. Mostly they pore over pre-Columbian charts, hoping to discover a new Vinland Map that gives their ancestors credit for getting there first. With tortuous reasoning that would have dismayed a medieval cabalist, some of the historians stretch so feeble a clue as a misspelled word to conjure up a whole flotilla of well-victualed galleons sailing bravely into the sunset. And almost invariably the zone of pre-Columbian discoveries takes in the Grand Bank and Newfoundland because of the richness of the fisheries.

Tantalizingly, a map drawn by Andrea Bianco in 1436 shows an island that could be Greenland, and, printed on the seas to the west about where the Grand Bank should be, is the single word "stokfis," only a small variation on the word used by many North European languages for dried cod. And even more striking, an island where Newfoundland should be is labeled "Isla Stokafixa," or Codfish Island, perhaps a better name for the place than the outmoded one it bears.

Virtually all charts published in the last few years before the Columbus voyage show beyond the Azores an island called Antille. Historians puzzle about the meaning of the name, but I find an easy clue in the Portuguese *ante ilha,* meaning "fore-island," an island on the road to somewhere else, which name fits Newfoundland as well as a hundred other sites. Regardless of the identity of the original Antille, the charts strongly suggest that long before 1492 somebody, probably a Portuguese sailor from the Azores colony, got as far into the New World as Columbus, who after all saw no more than the *ante ilha* of the continent on his first trip.

In 1476 a joint Danish-Portuguese expedition commanded by the famous pirate Diderik Pining and piloted by the Dane John Scolous sailed west. João Vaz Cortereal, grandfather of the Portuguese navigator immortalized by the statue in St.

John's, represented his king. The expedition reached what Cortereal called Land of the Codfish, and so Portuguese historians are pleased to credit their countryman with discovery of Newfoundland, though historians from other lands remain skeptical.

Not completely by coincidence, many skeptics prefer to find the misty pre-Columbian Great Navigator among their own countrymen. A Basque historian of excellent reputation, for instance, labors mightily with charts and early whaling prints to put his seagoing ancestors on the Grand Bank a century and a half before Columbus. Papers in the publication of a Basque historical society (thoughtfully published in Spanish rather than the unspeakable Basque language) solemnly recount as fact the legend of a century-old Basque colony in Newfoundland abandoned the same year as Columbus' voyage. According to these reports, survivors of the colony, sick with scurvy, trying to return home over half-forgotten sea routes, reached the Canary Islands the same day as the *Pinta,* the *Nina,* and the *Santa Maria* did on their outward voyage. The Basques told Columbus full details of the lands across the sea, but, alas, their accounts died among Spaniards who were not above suppressing the story and stealing the glory for their own fleet.

Even after the era of incontestable documents, details remain maddeningly vague, and patriotism still triumphs over reason.

On St. John's Day in 1497, the first British expedition to the New World, led by a Venetian sailor named John Cabot, sighted something. His son Sebastian many years later said he had accompanied his father and could flatly state that the land discovered was Newfoundland. Spaniards and Portuguese scoffed at his claim, though their testimony is tainted not only by their patriotic preference for an Iberian discoverer, but also by the fact that the Newfoundland fisheries had by then become valuable prizes.

But even the English repudiated Sebastian. In 1521 when the king asked the Draper's Company of London to finance Sebastian's expedition to the codfish islands, they answered:

> *And we thynk it were sore adventour to joperd shipps w$^t$ men & goodes unto the said Iland uppon the singuler trust of one man, callyd as we understond, Sebastyan, which Sebastyan, as we here say, was never in that land hym self, all if he makes reporte of many thinges as he hath hard his ffather and other men speke in tymes past.*

Trying to reconstruct the true landfall of Cabot's voyage, historians have picked a dozen sites from Nova Scotia to Labrador and some, of course, have included Newfoundland, but with little certainty.

Regardless of the exact site of landfall, Cabot almost certainly found the great fisheries of the Grand Bank, and his excited English seamen spread word of the fabulous riches of the western ocean throughout the West Country of England on their return.

Like a good patriot, Lorenzo Pasquaglio of Venice, then living in Bristol, England, wrote to his brother back home that he had witnessed the return not of a British expedition but of a Venetian who had seen the mainland home of the Great Khan 700 leagues away — a remarkably accurate estimate of the distance to the New World, by the way, considering the imprecise navigation of the day.

The following day Raimondo de Soncino wrote from Bristol to the Duke of Milan that a Venetian

> *has found two very large and fertile new islands. . . . This Messer Zoane Caboto, as a foreigner and a poor man, would not have gained credence, had it not been that his companions, who are practically all English and from Bristol, testified that he spoke the truth. This Messer Zoane has the description of the world in a map and also in a solid sphere, which he has made, and shows where he has been. [Both map and sphere long since lost.] . . . They assert that the sea there is swarming with fish, which can be taken not only with the net but in baskets let down with a stone, so that it sinks in the water . . . These same English, his companions, say that they could bring so many fish that this kingdom would have no further need of Iceland, from which place there comes a very great quantity of fish called stockfish.*

So even the reporters on the scene at Cabot's return could not agree if he had found island or mainland. But it mattered little, for it was the report of the great fishery which excited Europe.

Everybody agrees that Gaspar Cortereal led a three-ship Portuguese flotilla to the east coast of Newfoundland in 1501. The admiral and his flagship disappeared at sea, but the other two ships returned with kidnapped Indians described by the

Venetian ambassador as light-skinned and green-eyed. And they confirmed the Bristol sailors' tales of the teeming fisheries. For 75 years the Portuguese acted as though they owned the island, with no protest from the British.

Undaunted by the fate of Cortereal and of Cabot, who vanished on his second voyage to the great fisheries, hardy sailors of the maritime and fishing nations flocked to the dangerous seas along the Newfoundland coast. Place names in Portuguese, Basque, and French proliferated along the coast, and many remain today, though they have suffered strange alteration on the modern Newfoundlander's Anglo-Saxon palate. The sense of Baie d'Espoir, for instance, has been turned inside out, to Bay Despair.

Within a few years of Cortereal's voyage, 500 ships from France alone regularly fished on the banks, in addition to the uncounted numbers of Portuguese, Spanish, Basque, and English boats.

At first fishermen came from Europe in the spring, dried their catch ashore during the summer, and sailed home in the autumn. Laws even forbade permanent settlement on the island. But gradually fishermen deserted the homebound fleet, and clandestine colonies established themselves, not only in St. John's but at the head of virtually every fjord around the 6,000 miles of shoreline.

Life was hard in those outports. The winter diet was hardtack, salt fish, and fat back pork, a combination still boiled together to make "fish and brewis." (Even today island restaurants keep a pot of brewis simmering the year around as a matter of course, and a nourishing dish it is on a cold, foggy day, though the lack of vitamins may explain why many islanders assume they will wear false teeth from early adulthood.)

The outporters livened their monotonous diet and daily drudgery with prodigious dosages of home-brewed rum and beer made of spruce branches. Drunkenness was commonplace, and the towns were forever burning down because of some sot's carelessness with fire. And yet the islanders survived.

Visitors not hardened to the harshness of island life did not always do so well. In 1536 the English crews of two ships stranded on the island's south coast exhausted their stores of salt meat and hardtack. On shores where the hardy islanders fattened over the same winter and spring, the sailors over-looked the fish in the teeming waters and relied instead on gulls' eggs and bear meat till even that fare failed. After the shipwrecked sailors had seized a French ship and sailed back to England, one of the survivors frankly confessed how they had managed to escape starvation.

"If thou wouldest needes know, the broyled meate that I had was a piece of a man's buttocke."

After three-quarters of a century of neglect by home governments of all the fishing nations, the island suddenly became a prize worth fighting over when Sir Humphrey Gilbert in 1583 sailed an English flotilla into St. John's harbor and claimed the area for Queen Elizabeth. The town then numbered less than 50 wooden houses, but trade must have been good, for the merchants were able to offer the explorer salmon, trout, codfish of course, lobster, bread, biscuits, marmalade, and even wine. The fishermen and merchants were an unruly lot, and Sir Humphrey tried to impose government on the anarchical community. Almost immediately after his departure, the city fell back into chaotic misrule. Sir Humphrey, by

**35**

the way, suffered the common fate of early explorers in those troubled seas. On the homeward voyage, his ship went down with all hands in a storm.

Although life on the banks and the island was harsh, times were even harder for the poor back home in England, apparently, for in 1600 Richard Hakluyt, the geographer, wrote:

> *If we would behold with the eye of pity how all our prisons are festered and filled with able men to serve their country, which for small robberies are daily hanged up in great numbers, even twenty at a clap out of one jail (as was seen at the last assizes at Rochester) we would hasten and further, every man to his power, the deducting of some colonies of our superfluous people into those temperate and fertile parts of America, which, being within six weeks sailing of England are yet unpossessed by any Christians, and seem to offer themselves unto us, stretching nearer unto her Majesty's dominions than to any other part of Europe.*

John Guy, with permission of King James, tried to set up a permanent community at Cupids in 1610. Though the clandestine colonists hidden at secret outports held on to life, the Cupids venture failed, partly because of open warfare between permanent settlers and the summer fishermen from the homeland.

Among the adventurers, merchants, remittance men, honest fishermen, and ruthless pirates on the streets of St. John's walked explorers who used the island as a jumping-off place for trips along the unknown mainland coast. Most famous of them was Captain John Smith. One day the Virginia-bound soldier was approached by an Indian who introduced himself as Squanto. He claimed to know the coastal waters well, for he was an exile from the mainland hundreds of miles to the south, kidnapped by an early explorer of New England. He had spent his adolescence in the household of the Lord Chief Justice of England. Captain Smith hired him as a guide with a promise to put him ashore when they reached his home village.

But Captain Smith and his flagship were forced to turn back, so Squanto transferred to another vessel in the flotilla to continue down the coast. The captain treacherously kidnapped him again, however, and sold him with 22 other Indians on the slave market in Málaga, Spain.

Somehow, the stubborn Indian escaped his captors after a year in Spain and even rescued his friend Samoset, an Abenaki sagamore from Maine. They stowed away on a ship, and once out of the harbor they worked their way back to England. From there Squanto contrived to get to Newfoundland again, shipped out on another exploring expedition, and reached his home after 11 years of exile. But his homecoming was a bitter tragedy, for he found only the scattered bones of his people. His tribe had been wiped out by smallpox picked up from an earlier explorer's crew. He attached himself to the retinue of Massasoit, chieftain of a powerful nearby tribe, till the day his friend Samoset came to tell him that Englishmen were landing at the site of his old home village.

Squanto entered American history then as the Indian who deserted his own people to help the Pilgrims survive their first dangerous winter on the harsh New England coast. Governor

William Bradford in his report freely granted that his colony would have perished except for the guidance of the woodland Indian who had twice lived in Newfoundland during his strange wanderings around the North Atlantic basin.

France and England fought in Newfoundland waters the first skirmishes of the vast conflict for empire that would wrack North America. Victory came to the British partly for the odd reason that the sun shines feebly on the British islands. Unable to make salt by evaporation of seawater, English fishermen tended to work inshore waters so they could preserve the catch by drying their fish on raised platforms ashore. The French, with large stores of cheap salt available from their sunny southlands, fished more often on the banks and salted their catch at sea to preserve it for the voyage home. Gradually, through a long series of raids and reprisals, a tedious history of seesaw contention that must weary the Newfoundland schoolboy, the English drove out the French and took undisputed possession in 1763.

St. John's library offers a superb collection of historical documents about the squabbling between England and France, but the century-long affair is best summarized in a tattoo performed on summer Sunday afternoons at Signal Hill by a military company dressed in eighteenth-century uniforms. Firing old smoothbore muskets and muzzle-loading cannon, the soldiers form hollow squares, deploy into skirmish lines, and reform for bayonet attack in a simulated repulse of invading French.

At the library I found several eyewitness reports of conditions in eighteenth-century St. John's that made me wonder why anybody wanted it.

In the rococo doggerel considered fashionable in eighteenth-century English society, a certain B. Lacy, 13 years after the British take-over, reported on his visit to the island.

*Most that inhabit are a frightful Tribe,*
*Whose Characters I cannot well describe;*
*Who, like Siberians, lonely here reside,*
*And, in a willing banishment, abide.*
*It is this sottish People's common use*
*To warm their Veins with an infernal Juice,*
*Both men and women do this Liquor choose,*
*And rarely keep the Bottle from their Nose.*
*In both those Harbours many, I dare say,*
*Do drink some Quarts of Spirits in a Day*
*For with confounded Rum they ever stink . . .*

After a brief grapple with the local drink, a dark-hued rum appropriately labeled "screech," I doff my hat to those hardy pioneers who could down "some Quarts" of the stuff every day and still go about the backbreaking job of catching and splitting cod.

Clearly homesick for the manicured lawns and gardens of England, Mr. Lacy even condemns the island scenery:

*Numbers of craggy rocks hang o'er the sea*
*Yielding an horrid prospect from each Bay . . .*
*No painful Peasant breaks up this hard Ground,*
*Nor scarce a Blade of Grain can here be found . . .*

This is a patent libel on a land, which, for all its rugged coasts and interior wastelands, is blessed with some of the world's most breathtaking scenery. Mr. Lacy clearly allowed his disapproval of island morals to cloud his vision.

For a journalist there are few pleasures greater than stumbling across a good reporter writing truly and well about how it was several centuries ago. Such a reporter was Sir Joseph Banks, the great British naturalist, who kept a journal of his plant exploration tour of the island in 1766.

St. John's by then had grown to 300 houses sheltering 750 men and 350 women and children over the winter. On the entire island, he guessed, as many as 10,000 stayed permanently after the summer fishermen sailed home — most of them Irish who had fled religious persecution by the English in the homeland and hated the government of the Sassenach.

Along the coast away from government headquarters at St. John's, Sir Joseph was scandalized to find every harbor full of French ships illegally fishing inshore waters and trading with the Eskimos. But the French were well armed, the Irish outport people far more friendly to them than to their own government, and so the English found it convenient to look the other way.

Sir Joseph even found much to admire in the Norman and Breton fishermen. In a confession extraordinary for an English gentleman, Sir Joseph conceded that the French were cleaner than the English.

"Their stages are . . . sweeter or rather less stinking, for either theirs or ours would turn an Englishman's stomach who had not been inurd to them by degrees as we were.

"In the French stage is a little scaffolding on which the people lay their boughs and to which they swing their hammocks while our people are lying about the stage in little cabbins which in England would be thought too bad for pig sties."

He noted with approval that the French all sang as they

worked instead of toiling in sullen silence like the English. The ships' officers split the fish and passed them to the sailors for further processing. Because of their rank, they wore splendid uniforms even as they worked, so they protected their clothing by standing inside a case of bark.

"Into this they creep & putting on sleeves & large wollen gloves split the fish in a manner without touching it."

He described the fisherman's standard fare of boiled hard-tack, salt meat, and dried cod, but called it "chewder" rather than its modern name of fish and brewis. And unlike the testy Mr. Lacy who could find nothing good to say about the island or islanders, he quite correctly called the chewder "when well made a luxury."

Sir Joseph had an epicurean bent, for he recorded in full the recipe for making spruce beer, a curious beverage still brewed in the backlands by the occasional old-timer.

*Take a copper that contains 12 gallons, fill it as full of the boughs of black spruce as it will hold pressing them down pretty tight, fill it up with water, boil it till the rind will strip off the spruce boughs which will waste it about one third, take them out & add to the water one gallon of melasses. Let the whole boil till the melasses are disolved. Take a half hogshead & put in 19 gallons of water & fill it up with the essence. Work with barm or beer grounds [yeast] & in less than a week it is fit to drink. From this liquor in itself very weak are made three kinds of flip called here callibogus, egg calli and king calli. The first by simply adding rum or brandy. Or gin if you cannot get either of the first . . . The second by heating the first with the addition of an egg, some sugar. The third king calli by adding spirit to the content of the copper as soon as it is ready to put into the cask and drinking it hot.*

Besides enduring the hardships brought by the harsh climate and the barren soil, the outporters lived in daily peril from the Indians and Eskimos.

"Our people who fish in those parts live in a continual state of warfare with them firing at them whenever they meet & if they chance to find their houses or wigwams as they call them plundering them immediately.

"They in turn look upon us in exactly the same light as we do them, killing our people whenever they get the advantage of them & stealing or destroying their nets wheresoever they find them.

"They are extremely dextrous in the use of their bows & arrows & will when pressd by an enemy take 4 arrows 3 between the fingers of their left hand with which they hold the bow the fourth notchd in the string discharge them as quick as they can draw the bow & with great certainty."

The Indians carved from their victims not only the scalp but all the face down to the lip. Sir Joseph reported seeing the scalp of a certain Sam Frye with features so clearly preserved that when fleeing Indians dropped the scalp in the snow a year after Sam's death, the pursuing party recognized their old comrade.

Although Sir Joseph found much to admire in the courage and hardihood of the islanders, he joined the fastidious Mr. Lacy in his opinion of the capital.

"For dirt and filth of all kinds, St. John's may in my opin-ion reign unrivald as it far exceeds any fishing town I ever saw in England . . . offals of all fish of all kinds are strewed . . . as everything here smells of fish so you cannot get anything that does not taste of it. Hogs can scarce be kept from it by any cane and when they have got it are by far the filthyest meat I ever met with. Poultry of all kinds, ducks, geese, fowls and turkies infinitely more fishy than the worse towne duck that ever was sold for a wild one in Lincolnshire. The very cows eat the fish offal and then milk is fishy. This last particu-lar indeed I have not met with myself but I have been assured it is often the case."

Fishermen extracted cod-liver oil for use by tanneries in those days by stuffing the livers into great vats and allowing them to rot away. The rancid flesh melted and the oil ran off into pans. St. John's kept many of the vats in the heart of town till the middle of the next century, so Sir Joseph probably had solid grounds for his complaints.

The aristocratic savant wondered at the mixed shabbiness and elegance of the local smart set.

"We were all invited to a ball given by Mr. Governor where the want of ladies was so great that my washer woman and her sister were there by formal invitation, but what sur-prised me the most was that after dancing we were conducted to a realy elegant supper set out with all kinds of wines & Italian liquors to the great emolument of the ladies who eat & drank to some purpose. Dancing it seems agreed with them by getting them such excellent stomachs."

A vicious system of government, surviving from the first lawless years of the Newfoundland fisheries, aggravated the harshness of life in the outports during the eighteenth century. By custom, the skipper of the first vessel to enter a harbor at the beginning of the fishing season automatically became the "fishing admiral" and governed that harbor for the rest of his stay. Drunken brutes of no education ruled with iron fist, throwing the permanent colonists off their own beaches, evicting them from the houses they had built for themselves, levying staggering fines for picayune infractions, doling out savage lashings and worse. Laws still forbade settlers to build houses within six miles of a shore and so gave corrupt and brutal fishing admirals sanction of what little government there was.

On the other hand, the centuries-old threat from the Indians was abating as immigrant Micmac Indians from the mainland and resident whites hunted the native Beothuks like vermin. After the turn of the century, British government took firmer hold of island affairs, replacing the fishing admirals as law in the outports, but even an enlightened governor like Admiral Gambier could not prevent the merciless slaughter of the tribe's remnants. One Indian woman was hacked to pieces and the morsels paraded with glee through English villages. Admiral Gambier protested with genuine anguish against his countrymen's barbarism, but a native-born aide coldly informed him of the hopelessness of his efforts.

"The people do not plan to civilize the Indian and hope to kill more in the future than they have in the past."

So reduced was the Indian threat that in 1822 the first white man was able to walk across the island, in two months, without being molested.

In 1823 two hunters surprised a Beothuk and shot him dead. Another Beothuk fled from a nearby wigwam and drowned trying to cross a river on thin ice. In the wigwam the hunters found a Beothuk squaw and two daughters. One of the girls, about 22 years old, who called herself Shanawdithit but was renamed Nancy, quickly adapted herself to city life. The other two women soon died. Nancy had great artistic talent and sketched excellent pictures of Beothuk woodland life. But when she went looking for her people she returned to report that Beothuk life was no more; she was the last of her tribe. She died in 1829.

Curiously, English writers in recent years have tried to relieve their embarrassment about the extermination of the Beothuks with the classic English maneuver — blaming it on the French. But they cannot simultaneously boast of having expelled the aggressive French from the island in 1763 and blame them for crimes of the nineteenth century.

With the abolition of the fishing admirals and the extermination of the Indians, island life should have eased, but disaster struck in 1846. In St. John's a glue pot boiled over and set fire to a cabinetmaker's workshop. Flames spread rapidly through the city's wooden houses. Vats filled with cod-liver and seal oil burst and poured rivers of flame into the harbor, setting fire to anchored ships. That night 12,000 homeless islanders camped on the hills around and watched an immense bed of embers glow where their city had stood that morning.

No less tough than the outporters, the city folk began rebuilding immediately, but a hurricane blew up and carried away the half-built houses. Ships bearing relief food from Europe and America parted anchor cables and grounded on the storm-lashed beach. One of the churches which had survived the fire was blown off its foundations.

But next morning the islanders patiently gathered the pieces and began to reassemble them —

Only to watch the city burn to the ground again in 1892.

Worse than the great fires was the collapse of Newfoundland's banks in 1894. Business was paralyzed, savings vanished, money was worthless. Newfoundland suffered from the bank failure until recently. Foreign investors feared to put money into island ventures, and so work remained scarce, the poor lived with the constant fear of starvation, and many islanders spent years without handling $100 in cash. Hundreds contrived to live on a government dole of six cents a day.

Because the island is the point of the New World closest to the Old, it continued to be a major link between America and Europe.

Marconi received the first transatlantic radio message on Signal Hill outside St. John's in 1901. A trio of United States Navy seaplanes took off from Trepassey in 1919, and a single survivor made it to Lisbon on May 27 — the first airplane to cross the Atlantic.

A few weeks later two British pilots, Captain John Alcock and Lieutenant Arthur Whitten Brown, flew from St. John's to Ireland in 16 hours, the first men to cross the Atlantic nonstop.

Roosevelt and Churchill met aboard a warship in Placentia Bay in August, 1941, to sign the Atlantic Charter and reaffirm the principles of the Four Freedoms proclaimed earlier by Roosevelt. During World War II, the island became an "unsinkable" aircraft carrier, with air bases at Gander, Torbay, Harmon, and Argentia. For many years after the war, till transatlantic planes stretched their range so they could make the ocean in one hop from New York, transatlantic flights stopped at Newfoundland for refueling.

Today most planes bypass the island and fly instead over the Grand Bank. Far below still crawl the fishing boats manned by a breed of men toughened through almost five centuries of storm, snow and ice, shipwreck and starvation. Barnacled timbers from hundreds of fishing craft litter the floor of the bank. Each year steel plates of modern trawlers join the vanished sailing craft on the ocean floor, and the bones of another generation of seamen dissolve into minerals sustaining the teeming life around them. But fishing is the only life the sailors know; and when the call goes out on the island and in Portugal, Spain, France, Russia, Poland, East and West Germany, even far-off Romania, the sailors go down to the sea in ships to do business in great waters.

# On the Island

Blowing up from the southeast in spring, the warm breath of the Gulf Stream feels the shock of winter-chilled Cape Race and drops its load of moisture. The fog probes inland, shrouding ponds and bogs, spruce and birch woods in a gentle mist that quickens reawakening life for another brief summer of struggle for survival. And fishermen repair their dories and mend their nets to be ready when the great schools come from the banks to spawn.

*Perched on the cliff just inside St. John's harbor mouth, inshore fishermen huddle together in their colony called The Battery, stoutly resisting efforts of well-meaning reformers to move them to more comfortable quarters. For four and a half centuries, their ancestors have fished from outports like this, hanging precariously to the face of the steep escarpment that rings most of the island. Turning their backs on the unproductive land, they have taken their boats out to harvest the codfish come from the open sea to the sheltered island waters to spawn. Harsh as it is, it's the only life they know or want.*

To the young outport swain, his boat is his hot rod, his jalopy, his pride, and his joy. All week, his boat takes him to the hard school of the sea. Sundays his boat takes him a-courting, and the tune of its engine, the shine of its paint, the smartness of his seamanship tell for or against his suit among the water-wise maidens who face a lifetime of dependency on the boating skill of their men.

For the sake of the homely cod, British redcoats and French marines fought long and hard over Newfoundland and the surrounding waters. Now, far from the meadows of green Normandy and the orchards of Brittany sleep the Frenchmen who left home to serve the fleet of fishermen working the banks from the island colony of St. Pierre and Miquelon, last foothold of imperial France in North America. Under the long hours of daylight during the brief summer, flowers bloom over the exiles' graves in a profusion as luxuriant as the summer pasturelands of their distant French homeland

Like a giant anchored factory ship, Newfoundland offers a stable platform for processing the riches of the sea. On flakes and stages, outporters split cod as they have for centuries. And Japanese butchers teach islanders to cut whales into gargantuan steaks.

In spring as the water over the banks warms, vast schools of capelin seek the gravel beaches of Newfoundland. The males wait along the littoral; the females school out to sea. When they are ready, females swim singly toward shore and are caught between a pair of males for the ride to land. Squeezed between their partners, the females lay their eggs in such numbers that the beach becomes springy to the step, like a mattress. Hordes of predators, including man, gorge themselves on the swarming capelin but cannot deter their single-minded urge to spawn.

In early summer seabirds in uncountable millions lay their eggs on the bare rocks of St. Mary's shore and the islands of Witless Bay. Inland, the beaver feasts on tender young poplar saplings, the first fresh green bark since last winter's first freeze drove the tree's sap and the beaver under the surface for shelter.

*Lured by the glamour of city life on the mainland, the young are deserting the outports, but a few hardy souls hang on, pitting muscle and seafaring skill against the cruel sea, as their ancestors have for centuries. But stay-at-homes may be learning a dying craft, for factory ships are depleting inshore waters and American dollars are changing the processing of cod from splitting and drying to packaging of frozen fillets and sticks. This boy's career on the stages and flakes may be short.*

# 3

# The Sailor Ashore

*Home is the sailor, home from the sea . . .*

Only slightly larger than Ohio, Newfoundland nevertheless has a coastline so deeply indented that if it could be stretched out straight like a string it would reach from New York across North America, through San Francisco, across the West Pacific, through Honolulu, out the Hawaiian chain through the farthermost island, and another 700 miles to the remote Pacific bank of the French Frigate Shoal. And virtually the entire Newfoundland population, more than half a million islanders, lives on that strand, leaving the stunted forests and bogs of the interior almost uninhabited. It is the rare islander who does not look at the sea daily and listen to the crash of surf on the rocks nightly. The mewing of seabirds awakens him at dawn, and the moaning of foghorns lulls him to sleep in foggy darkness.

Almost half the islanders live on the Avalon Peninsula because it lies closest to the bank fisheries. But even that comparatively dense population lives within sight of the sea, either in the capital at St. John's or in fishing villages, the outports which snuggle in the shelter of every cove and creek of the jagged coast. Except for the 100,000 citizens of the capital and 27,000 in the paper mill town of Corner Brook on the western side of the island, most of the islanders pass their lives in 1,300 fishing villages and make their living on the sea. Nine out of ten of the outports number less than 500 inhabitants, fewer than graduate annually from even a small city high school on the mainland.

Names of the outports fascinate outsiders. Some make a wry comment on outport life — Bad Bay, Bleak Island, Misery Point, Famish Gut, Bareneed, Breakheart Point, and Empty Basket. But the outporters keep their sense of humor, for Ha Ha Bay is answered by Bleak Joke Cove. Perhaps the love of screech explains Lushes Bight and Little Hooping Harbor. After the ingenuity of the islanders in thinking of place names for almost 1,300 outports had been exhausted, the outporters fell back on the obvious, coming up with Nameless Cove and Harbor Harbor.

Mass immigration stopped long ago (the major export is no longer codfish but young islanders gone to the mainland looking for the richer life of the city), so the composition of the populace has frozen. A foreign-born islander is a rarer fish than an albino cod, and nine out of ten of the native-born islanders descend from the Irish and the English immigrants of generations past.

Inbreeding for generations has whittled down the family names so that a few dozen fill most pages of the phone directories. In one of the outports of the province across the Strait of Belle Isle every family in town is named Stone. In some ports the Guys or Gushues make up half the town, in others it's the Costellos, Walshes, or Maloneys. The same inbreeding and lack of mobility leave one town overwhelmingly Catholic, the next almost entirely Anglican.

The Irish settled in St. John's and the rest of the Avalon Peninsula, and so the city's speech has the accents of County Cork. Northward up the coast, the speech is a Devonshire dialect of two hundred years ago. Everywhere the island speech is only dimly comprehensible to a mainlander on first arrival, and some of the outport dialects are almost impenetrable even to lifetime dwellers in St. John's.

My first morning in the capital, I rose before the sun to go fishing with a new-made friend named Cecil Garland. In the Hotel Newfoundland's elevator, the liveried bellboy struck up a conversation, for he was clearly curious why a mainlander would be stirring at such a heathen hour. During the descent of six floors we bandied questions and answers without exchanging an iota of information, for each of us needed a simultaneous translation headphone to understand the other's English.

Hanging to the side of a steep cliff on the north shore of St. John's harbor, the fisherman's section, called The Battery, imitates as closely as possible the ramshackle charm of a distant outport. Footpaths zigzag between wooden houses. Housewives come in first dawn light to draw fresh water from community taps. Split fish dry on flakes along the water's edge far below. The scent of breakfast fish and brewis and the occasional snatch of seaman's chantey sweeten the air.

Booted fishermen clumping down footpaths guided me to the wharf. There I met Cecil Garland, a powerfully built man of middle years, who was passing out to his eight-man crew the fresh cotton work gloves they expect to destroy during each daily sortie. After checking over my city man's costume, Cecil wordlessly handed me boots, oilskin, and so'wester. We boarded the boat and shoved off into the morning's mist.

Outside the harbor's narrow mouth, the boat heaved in a long ocean swell. Though I could scarcely stand without staggering, the sailors in their clumsy rubber boots jumped nimbly across the well of the boat from gunwale to slippery gunwale with no fear of falling.

Captain Cecil found the morning's weather fair by island standards.

"It be ca'm today, shocking ca'm."

At the first cod trap of the traditional Newfoundland design, the sailors heaved mightily on the nets, closing the circle and hauling up the bottom till it was only inches below the surface. But they cursed and dropped the net back into the water.

"Only a few tomcod," Cecil said, "not worth loading into the boat. Them draggers on the banks be killing the fish before they come to shore and we'll all starve to make them foreigners rich. If we ain't got fish in the Japanese net, we've wasted the morning, byes."

The Japanese net was an experimental design brought to

the island for testing by a Japanese salesman known to Cecil only as Mr. Moto.

"Bayn't his real name," Cecil said, "but you know how hard it be to understand them Japs and their English blather. But they do be good fishermen, and Mr. Moto's trap holds the fish what slip out of mine."

As the ring of the Japanese trap closed toward our boat and the bottom rose, Cecil squinted at the surface. He broke into a grin and called across the narrowing circle of water to a sullen youngster who was glumly helping handle the net from a dory.

"Not so lourd, bye, we cotched a load of fish this day. Heft the weight of them and look at the water boil from the fish's tails."

Soon even to my unpracticed eye, as the catch neared the surface, I saw the water boil like a teapot from the struggles of thousands of fish to escape. Between groans as they heaved upward on the net, the sailors made small whoops of delight over the boiling water.

"T'ousan's of fish, byes," Cecil shouted. "Ye'll all buy the wife a new dress."

When the fins of the top layer of fish broke the surface, the sailors sang out happy estimates of the catch. The range of guesses was astonishingly close, and nobody argued with the skipper when he said:

"Nine t'ousan' poun's, byes. A big load. Look yarry with the net so ye don't make a clobber."

The gasping fish slid in silvery cascades over the gunwale into the well amidships, and sailors jumped into the hold to spear strays on long-handled fish forks and throw them back into the squirming mass of cod. When they had tidied up the "clobber," all hands stripped off the work gloves and threw them into the sea.

On the way home, in spite of the good catch in the Japanese trap, the sailor talk was gloomy — or lourd, as the local speechway puts it. The huge factory ships of Europe's maritime nations, especially the huge Russian fishing fleet, were getting all the cod on the banks before they had a chance to make the spring migration to the shore, the fishermen said. The inshore fishing was a dying business, fit only for men too old to learn another trade.

"Last week the byes acrost the strayt fished the whole seven days but Sunday, of course, and the shares come to only 65 cents for every jackeen of the crew."

The Battery had come to full life by our return. Somebody was playing an accordion and singing of the hard life at sea, the low price of fish, and the high price of flour. Undaunted by the prospects, a young couple, only half-hidden around the corner of a boathouse, were billing and kissing in the thrilling preliminaries of that biological gavotte which invariably leads to household cares and a hungry family.

Cecil walked me back to town with a running commentary on the sociology of the waterfront — and after a morning's Berlitz-like total immersion in the island language, I understood fully half of what he said.

Towheaded moppets danced a jig on the deck of a stern trawler from Hull for the amusement of idling limeys. Near the galley of the immaculate French cable repair ship *Ampere,* a few sailors and technicians tasted a midmorning snack with that ineffable concentration of rapture only a Frenchman can bring to his provender. A disabled Soviet factory ship entering the harbor under tow of a stern trawler caused an outburst of Slavic speculation aboard a Russian water tender tied to the wharf.

At the post office, stocky Portuguese with curly jet hair and flashing teeth dropped trash into litter baskets marked *"Caixote do lixo"* as a courtesy to the first settlers on the island and the compatriots of Cortereal.

"The Russians don't mix with us Newfies," Cecil said. "The Poles and the Germans are friendlier. The Portuguese dorymen are perfect gents. But when the English laddies come ashore, byes, look out. A wise man'll sloo, for it's takin' the drop of drink and clinkin' and cloutin' and ballyraggin' the town to a clobber.

"When too many go to jail, the skippers round up the local byes and have them sail the trawler home."

The great foreign fleets using St. John's harbor fill the pockets of ship chandlers and provisioners, Cecil said, but their voracious nets are destroying the fishery, traditional base of outport life.

"Ask them at the hotel for haddock," he said, "ye'll have a fine surprise."

Haddock was on the menu, and the waitress cheerfully told me they had "t'ousan's o' haddock." But shortly she came back to report that the chef said he hadn't seen a haddock in "t'ousan's o' mont's." The haddock, it appeared, was the first casualty of the savage assault on the bank fisheries by foreign trawlers. So I settled on a dish of f'ippers, the forepaws of seals and an extraordinarily good delicacy.

On my way to visit the outports to see for myself what is happening there, I stopped first near Topsail, where tuna fishing sportsmen bring in their trophies for weighing. The procession of charter boats with their 400- to 900-pound catches impressed me, but the locals among the spectators seemed disappointed.

"It's a handsome day," said a wrinkled old fisherman, "but the water be too civil for the tuna, *cruel* civil."

Word flashed through the crowd that the capelin scull was on at Middle Cove, only 18 miles away. I followed the excited crowd.

From the top of a cliff overlooking the rocky beach at Middle Cove, I witnessed one of nature's most astonishing miracles.

The gentle surf was thick and black with fish. So dense was the school that waves were more fish than water and rolled in sluggishly. Along the edge of the sea, islanders cast nets, scooped up fish in buckets, grabbed them with bare hands, shoveled them into wagons and trucks, and carried loaded baskets to their automobiles. I joined the islanders on the beach to watch the strange and suicidal compulsion of the capelin to spawn.

Those dense banks of capelin lying just offshore were almost entirely males. Farther offshore the females rested and waited till they felt ripe. When ready for spawning, they left the main harem in small patrols and moved toward the surf line where a pair of waiting males locked each female between them and rode the surf into the beach. There the trio wriggled a shallow depression into the pebbles, deposited the female's eggs, and fertilized them. A following wave carried some of them back to sea, but not all. In places the windrow of stranded capelin was three-feet deep and a quarter-mile long. The beach was half-pebble and half-egg to a depth of 18 inches, and the footing was springy.

A large powerboat that was trying to loop a bar net around part of the silvery horde moved slowly, plowing through an almost solid mass of the fish. Bonfires sprang up along the beach, and fishermen fried selected male capelin to a crisp golden brown. A red-haired father invited me to join his carrot-topped brood at the feast, and the six of us — four of us children at that — made away with 100 of the succulent little fish. The rest of his catch my host was taking home to salt as dog food, for use during the winter, and to dry for his family's table.

Much of the 11 million pounds caught on island beaches each June and July is frozen by the government to sell later in the season as bait for codfish long-liners, the fishermen who still follow the ancient practice of catching cod on long lines of baited hooks. Farmers plow the rest into their fields as fertilizers. Agricultural scientists say that what little fertility the thin island topsoil has comes from centuries of composting it with capelin.

Right behind the great capelin scull came the predators, the seabirds, flounders, perch, codfish, and squid that prey on the capelin while they are distracted by their single-minded frenzy to spawn.

Just 35 miles away in Conception Bay in Holyrood, each summer squid crowd into a cove so thickly you could not put your hand between them. In dozens of boats on the bay, fishermen of all ages turned cranks of a squid-jigging machine, a kind of wheel turning a conveyor belt armed with barbless hooks which poured a continuous stream of foul-hooked squid into the boat. As each squid emerged from the bay it squirted a violent stream of seawater and ink over fisherman and boat, so the squid-jiggers wore oilskins and so'wester under a cloudless sky.

One tireless 14-year-old boy cranked 10,000 pounds of squid into his boat the day I visited Holyrood.

Squid are sold for codfish bait. Except during times of the direst famine in the past, the islanders have not eaten squid, but experts at the fisheries experiment station foresee an early change in attitude and predict the squid will become a table delicacy as it has in Japan, Greece, Spain, and the other maritime nations of the world.

So also with whale meat. On Trinity Bay at Dildo, 30 miles from Holyrood, I watched three Japanese whale butchers flense two baleen whales and carve the rich red flesh into enormous cubes for freezing and transport to their homeland. A Norwegian overseer predicted that one day Newfoundlanders will venture a taste and decide that whale meat is too good for export to strangers.

A slump in the price of whale oil after the Korean War caused the collapse of the Northwest Atlantic whale fishery, which did not revive till 1964. International regulations provide for only land-based whaling in those waters, which effectively limits practical whaling to Newfoundland. Because of restricted whaling, the stocks of all species, even the blue whale, the right and humpback, once thought beyond the point of no return on the road to extinction, have recovered in less than 20 years to all-time high populations, offering a possible replacement for at least part of the dwindling inshore codfish population.

On the advice of a St. John's newspaperman from Dildo, I went to Whitbourne to catch the Newfie Bullet, a narrow-gauge passenger-freight train that rambles from the capital through Foxtrap (where the conservative ladies who were against all forms of change attacked tracklaying crews with brooms and umbrellas till driven off by armed militia), through Tickle Harbor, Come-by-Chance, Goobies, and Gaff Topsail, to Port-aux-Basques. The run was more an all-day singing and picnic on the grounds than it was a serious passenger trip. Impromptu card games sprang up on all sides, and when a youngster brought out his guitar, the car rocked with salty ballads of the outports.

> *Come all you good people,*
> *I'll sing you a song,*
> *About the poor people*
> *How they get along.*
>
> *They'll start in the spring,*
> *Finish up in the fall.*
> *And when it's all over*
> *They've nothing at all.*
>
> *And it's hard, hard times.*

They tolled a sad ballad about the disappearance in 1912 of the good ship *Southern Cross,* with its 180-man crew ". . . a strong and vigorous race, some from St. John's and Brigus and more from Harbour Grace."

And to relieve the gloom, they switched to the song about the Kelligrew's soiree.

> *If you want your eyeballs straightened*
> *Just come out next week with me*
> *And you'll have to wear your glasses*
> *At the Kelligrew's soiree.*
>
> *There was birch rine, tar twine,*
> *Cherry wine and turpentine*
> *Jowls and cavalances,*
> *Ginger beer and tea*
> *Pig's feet, cat's meat,*
> *Dumplings biled in a sheet*
> *Dandelions and crackies' teeth*
> *At the Kelligrew Soiree.*

Most popular of folk tunes was *Squid Jiggin' Ground,* a rollicking number that warns landlubbers —

> *Now if ever you feel inclined to go squiddin'*
> *Leave your white shirts and collars behind in the town*
> *And if you get cranky without your silk hanky*
> *You'd better steer clear of the squid jiggin' grounds.*

A striking number of the jokes exchanged among the passengers concerned the classic Newfoundland yokel on his first visit to a sister in the States. The stories began with some variation of "She opened the door to his ring and there he stood grinning, every inch a Newfie with his blue serge suit on and yellow shoes, his cardboard suitcase in his hand and not a tooth in his head. . . ." And the stories continued with a merciless laugh at their own provincialism.

The conductor told me that along a western stretch of track the company hires a wind sniffer who several times daily tests the gale blowing down the mountainside to be sure it is not strong enough to blow the train off the track — a disaster the trainman solemnly assured me had happened just three years before. The breeze was a zephyr when we rolled into Port-aux-Basques.

# On the Banks

When the capelin come ashore to spawn, hard behind follow predators feasting on the little fish and each other in the complex chain of life, with man the final predator. At Holyrood hordes of squid chasing the capelin end as the prey of man.

Although born and reared in a land of perpetual sunshine, Portuguese fishermen after reaching manhood rarely see a summer sun except through a patch in the sempiternal fog that shrouds the island and the banks. The island fishermen have not even the memory of those long hot summers of childhood to warm them in the bone-chilling fogs that blow over the shoals and rocks where warm Gulf Stream and icy Arctic Current collide.

Inshore fishermen work their traps only from spring through fall, but the icy waters around the island retain the memory of bitter winter late into summer. Grotesque icebergs calved by Arctic glaciers float southward on the Arctic Current to infest the island waters, perils to navigation but also bearers of nutrients for the phytoplankton that sustain the food chain of the banks.

*In dories lifted from nests on the mother ship, Portuguese tend handlines at Virgin Rocks, keeping one eye on the white ship's ghostly loom, for to be lost in the fog is to die. The days of the Great White Fleet are numbered; even the hardy Portuguese cannot compete with the mechanized stern trawler like the* Atlantic Peggy *of St. Mary's, Newfoundland.*

Each recovery is like a cast of dice, and fishermen risk drowning to hurry the net over the sternway and check their luck. But often the catch is a barnacled spar from an old wreck that means hours of repair and no pay.

*"When a fisherman is idle, he mends his nets,"* says an island proverb. And diligent work by flying wooden *"needles"* weaves a mesh cunningly sized to trap only marketable fish like this whopping 7,000 pounds of flounder.

Once thought inexhaustible, the fisheries show signs of flagging under the assault of Communist bloc factory ships which rarely leave the banks. Fresh water, food, spare parts, movies, library books and, above all, relief crews arrive by tender. Freighters carry off packaged fish and fish meal. So the banks fisheries, though still immense, are never allowed to rest and recover.

# 4

# Out to the Banks

*Sand strewn caverns cool and deep,*
*Where the winds are all asleep;*
*Where the spent lights quiver and gleam;*
*Where the salt weed sways in the stream;*
*Where the sea-beasts, ranged all round*
*Feed in the ooze of their pasture-ground.*

Only yesterday in geological time Newfoundland was not just close to the Grand Bank but indeed was part of the bank. Even since modern man has walked the earth, the island was submerged. But today the trawlers which work the banks must sail hours to reach those shallow breeding grounds where hot and cold rivers in the sea collide. At Marystown on the Burin Peninsula of the south coast of Newfoundland, I boarded the *Atlantic Jane* for a cruise to the bank. The stern trawler was making its seventh trip to sea. A modern 153-footer, it represents the future of island fishing.

Light poured down from a crystal-clear sky while Captain Martin O'Keefe took the trawler across Mortier Bay. Rocks lining the narrow harbor mouth were clearly visible under the rare sunshine, but from force of habit developed over years of navigating in fog, the skipper steered as much by radar as by sight. Ten minutes outside port, fog closed a woolly curtain around us, cutting visibility in five minutes from 20 miles to 50 feet.

Like a blind man indifferent to daylight or dark, the skipper ignored the fog and piloted with instruments — including a 48-mile and a 12-mile radar, automatic pilot and manual wheel, gyroscopic compass repeater and magnetic compass, Fathometer and fish-finder, three two-way radios, piso pitometer, internal communication telephones, bullhorn microphone, control panel for the trawling winches, engine gauges, flag locker, barometer, radio direction finder, two lorans, and the all-important Decca Navigator Mark 12. Island sailors who can scarcely print their names read the Decca at a glance and confidently spot their position from memory of past readings. The crossing of Decca vectors has replaced traditional latitude and longitude coordinates for position finding among banks fishermen. The ship's clock, which must be split-second accurate for celestial navigation, was ten minutes fast and nobody cared.

Sailors bustled about the deck laying out gear. Although fog hid the sun, the fishermen carefully located south so they would not bring on bad luck by coiling rope against the sun. Swift hands plying wooden needles mended the net.

"When fishermen are idle, they mend their nets," the skipper said. "It's like knitting for women; it gives them something to think about while they talk."

The fog lifted and near the horizon the island was just barely in sight.

"That's Cape Pine and Trepassey Bay," the first mate said.

"Little town of St. Shotts there. High on the cliff I seen an anchor taller than a man. Joe Pitcher climbed through the eye of it. And nobody knows how it got there or why.

"Once a little boy was sailing with his father across Trepassey Bay when he sung out a little tune they had learned him on the beach:

> *There's hair on me head*
> *There's none on me toes*
> *There's woods on Cape Mutton*
> *There's none at the Poles.*
> *Back of Trepassey*
> *Lies all rocks and shoals.*

"And he reminded his old father like that of the dangers in the bay, so the father swung the ship out at the last minute and saved them all from drowning."

The broadcast band radio crackled a steady stream of public and private notices. Because of the isolation of the outports, Newfoundland radio is more a communication network than an entertainment medium.

"From Mrs. Senior at Spanish Room," the radio says. "Tell Mr. Grouchy to send me a hundredweight of potatoes. . . .

"The trawler reported lost last night has been found aground on the beach with 24,000 pounds of fish near Rose-Blanche. All hands are safe. . . ."

We steamed all night at 12 knots to reach the far side of the bank where the skipper had jealously guarded private knowledge of a great school of flounder. At midmorning the winches shuddered and groaned and the cables hummed as we payed out the net of the otter trawl, the two heavy wooden "doors" which act like submerged paravanes to hold the net mouth open, and 600 fathoms of cable to drag the rig across the bottom 200 fathoms below.

Two hours later we hauled up the first set, bulging with 6,000 pounds of gasping flounder and cod. Winches lifted the net over a hatch in the stern and poured the cascade of fish into the hold. The crew payed out the net and laid below to gut and clean the catch and pack it in ice.

Day and night we followed the monotonous routine made interesting for the sailors only by the fact that every load of fish was money in their pockets.

And over the two-way radios skippers gossiped interminably about the catch, shamelessly telling outrageous lies to hide the location of their favorite fishing grounds.

"We got 12,000 pounds on the last set," Captain O'Keefe said to a rival trawler. When the other fishermen sputtered with excitement about the size of the catch, Captain O'Keefe tried to calm him. "Don't believe a word of it. I'm blathering. We ain't catching enough to feed the ship's cat. The company won't be able to pay for the ice if luck don't change."

And every two hours the net was pulling up between 3,500 and 8,000 pounds to everybody's satisfaction. During the night a tremendous catch burst on deck and most of 15,000 pounds of fish slithered over the side. The next morning the skipper interrupted the monotony by calling up his rivals for another exchange of lies. As they whined about hard times and poor fishing, the ship jolted to a halt as though it had run up on a reef. The skipper dropped the radiophone, leaped for the winch controls, and payed out slack to keep the cables from parting. We had snagged the starboard paravane, or door, on a sunken ship, one of hundreds of ship skeletons paving the ocean floor on the bank, the debris of almost 500 years of tragedy at sea.

For an hour skipper and crew struggled to free the ship, twisting and hauling from different directions, lifting the sunken hull, and slamming it back to the sea bottom as the rolling sea heaved us about on the surface. Whenever the skipper put strain on the cable attempting to free us by brute force, he cleared the deck for fear the cable would part and behead anybody in its reach.

Suddenly the tension broke, the cable rode free. But we had to rig a spare door to replace the one which had stayed below on the sunken ship. For two hours, all hands worked with flying fingers to repair the tangled and shredded net.

The captain carefully noted his position on the Decca and filed the location of the wreck in a memory jammed with information about sunken hulls, boulders, and lost anchors.

"When we first come here draggin' in 1945," he said, "the bottom was covered with anchors, but we don't hit them often anymore. I think we hauled them all up. Plenty of wrecks though and more every year. I been lucky, for this is the first time I ever snagged one. And I'll never snag that one again."

Fifteen minutes later we scooped a submerged wreck down the mouth of the $2,500 net, which was carried away and lost.

That night the *Atlantic Jane* lost the spare net on another wreck and had to sail for home, but only after transferring me by dory to the sister ship *Atlantic Peggy*.

John Kelley, the acting skipper of the *Peggy*, could legitimately have looked at me askance as a Jonah, for on the first set after I boarded his ship, the net wound itself like a cocoon around a barnacled ship's timber and gave the crew an un-profitable morning of work with the needles. But the skipper was philosophical. "Once you put the net over the stern, you are never sure to see it again."

The sailors freed the timber and carried it to a pile of beams, whalebones, and salt-encrusted ship's hardware they had pulled from the net on earlier casts.

"Someday we're going to haul up the biggest ship that ever went down anywhere," the skipper said. "In 1912 the *Titanic* hit an iceberg right about where we'll be tonight and went down with 1,500 people. And 100 years ago the *Arctic* went down with more than 300 passengers. The idiot skipper was running full speed through a Grand Bank fog with only a little tin horn blowing. Of the 87 who survived, most were crew. Not a single woman or child was saved, mostly because the crew stole all the lifeboats."

Another sailor told about the bitter winter night in 1942 when the destroyer U.S.S. *Truxton* and the supply ship U.S.S. *Pollux* ran aground in a blinding snowstorm at Chamber Cove. Four sailors swam ashore, climbed the icy face of a 200-foot cliff, and walked to the Iron Springs mine looking for help. The miners rescued 168 of the stranded sailors, but 200 of their shipmates drowned.

The roster of historical disasters continued. But gradually talk shifted to personal experience with shipwreck. Every sailor in the crew had either survived a shipwreck himself or had lost relatives and former shipmates at sea.

"Captain Eddie Brewer went down last year with nine men in a breeze and a frost on Green Bank."

"And the *Iceland II* just last winter ran ashore on the

sockers above Louisbourg. All hands drowned, but it wasn't near so bad as some wrecks for they got most of the bodies."

"I seen side trawlers white with frost pulling in little cod frozen before they could gut them. That's how the *Blue Mist* was lost. I talked to the mate on the radio at nine o'clock. He said he'd call back at eleven, but nobody ever heard from them again. Turned over under a load of ice on the rigging."

The mate told of being run down by a Norwegian shark fisherman in a fog. But the Norwegian hit the trawler in the freshwater tank which simply spilled its load into the sea and held firm as an improvised cofferdam.

The sea tales multiplied as each sailor told of his own misadventures. Even the youngest told of losing his ship, a victim of its own door which punched a hole through the hull.

"The breeze was high and our dory was wallowing, because the boat was built for no more than three, and there was eleven of us and all our dirty laundry we was taking home for our wives to wash. The *Fortune Star* picked us off the Burgeo Bank just before the whole of us started yucking from the seasickness."

The *Acadia Sea Hawk* disappeared with 16 sailors, the *Cape Bonnie,* the *Red Diamond,* the *Reliance* — the list stretched on of ships lost just within recent months. For almost 500 years this tragic price has been wrung from the fishing fleet by the stormy Grand Bank. And still the sailors come from all around the Atlantic basin to work those dangerous seas.

The skipper stayed close to the radar, for half a dozen trawlers were working the area despite the blinding fog. And when the *Rupert Brand* broadcast a warning that its radar and running lights had broken down, the skipper of the *Peggy* was nailed to his radar till the blinded trawler had left for home.

When the last set had been poured into the hold and the ship turned homeward, the fishermen shaved for the first time in a week, changed clothes, and pomaded their hair, which had been "all mops and brooms" since the cruise began. They gathered about the wheelhouse, straining for the first glimpse of land, and sang out the names of capes and bays as they passed down our starboard side. Though the men had been standing eight hours on and four hours off for eight straight days, nobody improved the homeward run by napping.

"Used to be fish in the summer and fun in the winter," the skipper said, "but it's fish the year around now, so the lads have to grab their fun when they can."

For me, the landing meant only a transfer to the side trawler *Beinir,* a training vessel of the provincial fishery school, for a trip to inspect the foreign fleets.

When we sailed for the Grand Bank, Captain Gordon Harris used his radar not to shy away from ships but to lay the *Beinir* as close alongside as he could with safety so we could look over the operation. We passed through a flotilla of Russian craft — trawlers, cannery and refrigerator ships, freighters, water barges, machine shops, all the tenders necessary to keep a fishing fleet at sea for months, independent of home. The Newfoundland sailors muttered dark suspicions of the goings-on among the Russian fishermen.

"I watched a trawler work for 18 hours once," the helmsman said, "and he never once lifted his net. I think they lower a big vacuum cleaner and suck the fish out of the sea. And once the Russians have fished over the bank, you can forget that part, for there is no fish left."

74

The skipper took us down to Virgin Rocks, a part of the bank so shallow that seas sometimes break there and the last holdout of old-fashioned long-lining. When we came within ten miles of the rocks, the skipper slowed the *Beinir* and poked forward cautiously in the mist for fear of running over dorymen from the Portuguese White Fleet. The fog thinned briefly, and a ghostly white barkentine showed through the drifting mist. Scattered about the sea were 90 one-man dories, each one the home of a Portuguese fisherman for more than half of his life.

For 100 years, each March the fishermen have left Figueira da Foz, Viana do Castelo, Aveiro, Oporto, Furodouro, Póvoa de Varzim, Setúbal, Fuzeta — all the fishing villages of the Portuguese coast. They fit out the mother ships and sometime in April, after midnight mass at the Church of the Jerónimos at Lisbon, the fleet sails for the Grand Bank.

On the fishing grounds they rise at 3:30, toss off a ration of brandy, and await the captain's orders. If he decides the weather is safe for fishing, the dories shove off and the fishermen pay out line with 500 hooks set 6 feet apart. For 16 hours they tend that line, returning to the ship only to unload or when the sun is setting — or when the fog closes in, for a doryman lost on the bank is in serious peril. (Citizens of one of the world's sunniest nations, these Portuguese fishermen rarely see the summer sun after childhood.)

The hour was late when we arrived and the barkentine hoisted "Blue Peter," the recall flag, and sounded long blasts to help guide distant dorymen through the mist.

"The sailing ships and dories make a pretty sight," the skipper said, "but it won't last much longer. As fast as a sailing ship sinks or wears out, the Portuguese replace it with a modern trawler. We'll miss them in St. John's when they are all gone, for it's a big event every spring when they first arrive.

"We Newfies like the Portuguese, you know, because they are such perfect gents and let our kids join the game when they practice football on the dock. And we can always count on a good bargain swapping them bait, gloves, spare line, clothing, anything for wine and brandy.

"But where we're headed now is a paradise for that kind of deal. Let's go to France!"

And he promptly headed not east but west toward St. Pierre, a rocky little island 12 miles off the coast of Newfoundland and the last outpost of the French empire left in North America. The obscure little port became famous during the Prohibition era as the base of a vast smuggling operation. Damon Runyon wrote a story about American bootleggers in St. Pierre. What the islanders call *la fraude* brought great prosperity while the American madness lasted.

Even today with whiskey selling for stiff prices in government liquor stores on Newfoundland, *la fraude* helps the French island economy. Our helmsman was excited about going to the easygoing island and told how at Christmastime dragger-trawlers working the neighborhood of St. Pierre pass close to the port to buy liquor by the dram from peddlers in the high-ended dories typical of St. Pierre.

"If the Mounties hear a dragger has been into St. Pierre, they tear the boat apart looking for contraband whiskey, so the draggers just do business at sea, put the stuff over the side in an oil drum before entering port, then go out to pick up the drum in a small boat. They bury the bottles on the beach and don't go near them for weeks, for fear a Mountie is watching.

"Of course, the tourists are ruining the business and driving up prices. It's really just as cheap to go to the government store — but not as much fun."

The harbor and little city of St. Pierre are a delightful copy of a Breton seaport, but they were not always so. When the immense French sailing fleet of fishing boats was based on St. Pierre and codfish were still dried and salted in the old-fashioned way, fish dominated the scene.

A French visitor in 1886 recorded his impressions.

"St. Pierre is the land of the cod. Everything is based on cod. When you walk abroad you see cod everywhere and unfortunately you smell them. In the stores tools for fishing cod, along the docks salt for curing cod; on the wharves barrels for cod, in the streets codfishermen; everybody lives on the cod; if two persons are chatting, the tag of conversation you overhear in passing will contain the word cod, always cod, everywhere cod, nothing but cod. Ask 20 persons their opinion of St. Pierre and 19 will say it is an abominable place, a sterile rock.

"I hesitate to deny those accusations but I have to confess I don't find the island so terrible. It possesses that great virtue of men and places of not being banal, of having a physiognomy, an originality. I've seen it in a fog when it was not completely without charm."

Less charmed by St. Pierre in a fog were the thousands of seamen who have piled up on the coast of St. Pierre and its sister island Miquelon. In the lobby of the Hotel Ile de France, a chart shows the location of 343 wrecks along the shore, but the innkeeper assured me the map was grossly inaccurate and far behind the times.

"The bones of at least 500 ships are rotting on our beaches."

In the local museum are magnificent figureheads taken from stranded sailing vessels and a haunting idol carved by some unknown Polynesian from a coconut log and carried by unguessable adventures to this distant fogbound shore.

Four thousand Spanish sailors from the bank prefer the Latin ambience of St. Pierre to the Anglo-Saxon austerity of St. John's. A waterfront cafe displayed a sign reading *"Esta Noche Hay Baile con Orquesta."* The skipper of a *pareja* invited me aboard and shared a bottle of *rioja* wine with me as he explained the Spanish system of dragging an especially wide-mouthed trawl between a pair of ships to sweep the widest possible track across the bottom. We broke off the technical discussions to watch a soccer team from his crew soundly trounce rivals from across the dock. The Basques aboard had gone into town to play *pelota,* the ancestor of *jai alai,* at a fronton maintained by the city for the amusement of its Pyrenean visitors. The Anglos from Newfoundland put in a hard day shopping among the island's forbidden fruits.

Dinner at the hotel was superb, and the *carafon* of wine was bottomless. Afterward I went with the Newfie sailors — *les Nioufs* as the Frenchmen call them — to a nameless nightclub where a two-piece orchestra played the *bal musette* style of Paris in 1900 and fishermen danced in their rubber boots.

We tied up in St. John's just at sunrise. The customs officer who boarded the *Beinir* graciously accepted a drink from the captain's one permitted bottle while the crew slipped over the gunwale and sauntered innocently away in the dawn's early light.

# 5

# The End of the
# Age of Abundance

*The use of the sea and air is common to all; neither can a title to the ocean belong to any people or private persons, forasmuch as neither nature nor public use and custom permit any possession thereof.*

Queen Elizabeth I

For almost 500 years after the Basque whalers or Portuguese explorers or whoever it was discovered the fisheries of the Newfoundland Banks, sailors from most of the maritime nations around the North Atlantic basin had worked the waters hard without making appreciable inroads on the enormous stocks of fish. But in 1955 a Russian fisheries research vessel showed up on the banks, and the age of abundance ended. By 1960 the first Soviet factory ship appeared on the banks, and today at least 500 Soviet trawlers plus a flotilla of tenders work there. Poland and East Germany have sent similar fleets. Romania is sending trawlers through the Black Sea and the Mediterranean and across the Atlantic to fish the banks. Cuba is building trawlers, and Soviet technicians are training a corps of trawler fishermen. Even Japan occasionally sends trawlers and factory ships across the vast reaches of the Pacific and through the Panama Canal to fish the Northwest Atlantic.

The new ships fish over the stern with murderously efficient otter trawls, making possible year-around dragging. But even the ordinary otter trawl, efficient as it is, may soon be obsolete. Fishery experts suspect that the secretive Russians use lights to attract fish to the net or the vacuum scoop. Also they have learned that in a magnetic field fish will orient themselves to the lines of flux and then swim toward the anode. An electrode before a trawl net will guide schools of fish into the mouth. Electric gear can fence in schools of fish and stun or kill them. Eventually, the electric fence may eliminate nets entirely.

Traditionally, fishermen hunted the cod during the spring and summer, and the stock wintered in deep waters unmolested. The old-fashioned side trawler had to turn broadside to the weather so the fishermen could take in the net over the lee rail. They had to process the catch on the open deck exposed to the harsh Atlantic weather. Winter storms in the Northwest Atlantic cut down sharply the number of days a side trawler could work with even the minimal safety the hardy banks fishermen required. But invention of the stern trawler permitted the skipper to head into the wind, take in the net over the stern, and dump the set below decks where the crew could process the fish out of the weather. So the fishing season continued through the winter.

Even the stern trawler, however, had to go to port occasionally to unload its catch, do routine maintenance, and, above all, give the sailors a day or two of rest. For the toughest of fishermen, even the incredibly hardy Portuguese long-liners, must go ashore once in a while. The Russians have changed all that. They send out not only trawlers, but all the tenders necessary to keep them on station. They process the catch at sea and put the frozen or canned fish and dried fish meal aboard a freighter headed for home. Relief crews rotate duty on the banks, but the fishing vessels themselves stay on station the year around.

After the Russians arrived on the Newfoundland Banks, the total catch jumped from 861 million pounds to 1,046 million. Some 2,000 ships and 50,000 sailors of at least 14 nations were working ceaselessly on the fish stocks.

Within five years of that kind of intensive and unrelieved assault, the stocks began to show the strain.

Captain O'Keefe of the *Atlantic Jane* told me, "When I came fishing we'd fill the boat with haddock as fast as we could haul net. Then it was nothing to see 50 boats at once on the haddock grounds near the tail of the Grand Bank. Now you could fish for a month and not fill the net once. So the trawlers have scattered and fish now for flounder.

"And when we first turned to flounder we got 15,000 pounds a set. Now we're down to 3,500 a set, and the net is a little lighter every time we bring it up."

Fishermen are notoriously pessimistic, and fishing captains whine about their hard lot worse than football coaches to confuse and mislead the competition. But even the most conservative of the fishery scientists and regulating bodies agree with Captain O'Keefe about the shrinking stocks. In 1965 the Fisheries Research Board of Canada issued its first warning.

> *Recent years have seen major increases in man's attempt to exploit the world's fish resources and resulting increases in the total*

*yield. . . . Landings of species such as cod, haddock, and halibut, long most important to countries fishing in the Northwest Atlantic, have increased relatively little, or in local situations have even decreased in importance.*

The 21-nation Organization for Economic Cooperation and Development reported its concern about overfishing of cod stocks.

Officers of the International Commission for the Northwest Atlantic Fisheries — a 14-nation voluntary regulatory body called ICNAF for short — reported in 1966 that ". . . increasing fishing activity is already approaching or even beyond the level giving maximum sustained yield for the main cod and haddock stocks."

The ICNAF statistics showed for the first time an alarming development — a drop in pounds of fish caught per unit of effort.

Dr. Wilfred Templeman, eminent biologist of the Fisheries Research Board of Canada, reported the ominous fact that haddock huddled closer and closer together as their numbers were reduced by overfishing, leaving themselves vulnerable to intense fishing till so few are left they are no longer worth hunting.

"The haddock fishery of the Newfoundland area is in a critical condition. I foresee small landings over the next few years. Cod will be smaller, the reduced number of large cod will have more natural food, and line fishing with bait will become more uneconomic. . . . Increasing use of large-meshed nylon gill nets, which catch large cod throughout the fishing season, may significantly hasten the reduction in numbers of large cod and so make the autumn fishery unprofitable."

Those nylon gill nets, because they are virtually indestructible, have introduced a new hazard to fish stocks. When a gill net goes adrift by accident or in a storm, it continues to catch fish till their dead weight pulls the net to the bottom. The fish rot or are eaten by scavengers, and the net floats to the top again to catch another load of fish in an endless cycle.

For almost 500 years the codfish of the Northwest Atlantic yielded a substantial portion of the western world's protein. The Catholics of the Mediterranean countries fasted on cod during Lent. The armies of northern Europe kept strong and aggressive on cod. The poor sometimes went hungry, but true famine was rare and chronic protein starvation almost as rare. But the medical revolution after World War II made possible an alarming and worldwide jump in population, throwing a strain on all food supplies and especially on sources of animal protein. And the population boom has only started. Soon the teeming masses of Asia are going to cast about desperately for new sources of protein.

Population experts predict a world population of 6 billion by the year 2000. Food production must be tripled just to hold the present unsatisfactory level of nourishment.

A White House advisory committee warned in 1967 that, "The world food problem is not a future threat. It is here now and it must be solved within the next two decades."

The big pinch will be for animal protein. The main product of agriculture is carbohydrate. Most people live on cereals, potatoes, yams, cassavas, and other starchy vegetables which furnish only 1 to 12 percent of protein by weight. But a man needs 14 percent to stay strong and bright and fight off infections. Children and pregnant or nursing mothers need 16 to

85

20 percent. Children deprived of protein grow up dim-witted — if they grow up at all. Chronic protein deficiency causes half the deaths of children younger than five.

Merely increasing food production will not help. Eating more conventional foods with low protein content will make the diner fat but leave him as sickly and sluggish as before.

It is fashionable now to predict that relief will come from the sea. Scientists of the Food and Agriculture Organization of the United Nations lead the enthusiasts. They point out that presently only 10 percent of the world's protein supply comes from aquatic organisms. But Japan for centuries has fished 75 to 90 percent of its protein supply from the sea. The FAO scientists hope the rest of the world can do as well.

Most marine biologists remain skeptical that the sea can prevent the ghastly protein famine forecast for the next two decades. One scientific report pegged the world's sustainable catch at only slightly more than is already being taken.

The hitch in using the sea to feed the poor with present fishing methods lies in the hard economic reality that the rich get richer and the poor get poorer. The great customer of the banks fishery is the United States. Everybody except Russia — even Communist Poland — tries to sell on the American market for dollars. Traditionally, most cod has been dried or salted and shipped to the Mediterranean basin or the West Indies and Latin America, but the lure of the American dollar increasingly persuades fishermen to freeze fillets of cod and other popular species for sale in American supermarkets. And the few species acceptable to American palates — only a few dozen of the 25,000 known species are used directly or indirectly as food by man — already show signs of being overfished.

The FAO's bulletins pridefully cite the enormous growth of the Peruvian fisheries during the past decade — but fail to mention that most of the catch is the anchoveta, a little so-called industrial fish which Peruvians grind into fish meal and sell to America and other rich countries for poultry and cattle feed. True, the world catch in ten years almost doubled, but the percentage of fish used as human food dropped from 83 to 63 percent. The rest fed chickens and hogs. Or dogs and cats of the well-fed nations. And the children of the poor of Asia and Africa still die or grow up weak and dull for lack of protein, a situation the have-nots eventually will rebel against.

Increasing the catch on the Newfoundland Banks can be done only by going after unfamiliar species, some of them so hideous to American eyes that housewives would refuse to touch their flesh much less serve them. But the protein is there whether or not the fish are pretty, or even palatable. Ground up whole, dried, and fed to unfastidious chickens and hogs, the ugly fish are converted to graceful drumsticks and shapely pork chops. Fish meal is even fed to fish in farm ponds.

Some scientists and economists predict the world will soon have a cheap source of famine relief in fish protein concentrate, a tasteless, odorless powder added to cereals as a human protein supplement. FPC, as the concentrate is called, presently is made by grinding up red hake, a soft-bodied relative of the cod, and dissolving the whole mass — flesh, bones, scales, and all — in an isopropyl alcohol solvent. (Any edible fish besides hake would be suitable.) A three-stage extractor removes most of the moisture and oil content, and the whole fish comes out of the process as a dry cake containing as much as 85 percent animal protein. The cake is ground to a dry tan powder which keeps well under difficult conditions. From 100,000 pounds of raw fish, current methods yield about 15,000 pounds of FPC.

The use of FPC as a diet supplement in protein-hungry nations has its critics who argue that there are cheaper ways to provide animal protein. Nevertheless, science has conquered far tougher problems than making fish powder available at a practicable price. A few pilot plants already grind up thousands of pounds of fish daily and spew forth hundreds of barrels of FPC, but this production is almost certainly only the first trickle of what eventually will become a flood. Soon vast schools of fish will be converted whole into nourishing but gastronomically unexciting flour rather than being sliced into savory but wasteful fillets.

To protect present fishery stocks and the present method of processing selected species into frozen flesh, the 14-member countries of ICNAF regulate the size of net mesh so that fish can escape to grow large. Big fish, of course, yield more fillets than small fish. Nobody in his right mind would try to slice fillets from a sardine. And fillets are what bring dollars, so big mesh it is.

Small fish, however, are much more efficient grazers than big fish, and some scientists are beginning to doubt if the hungry world will long allow the rich nations to indulge themselves in the wasteful practice of netting only big fish.

Dr. Lloyd Dickie of the Bedford Institute of Oceanography in Dartmouth, Nova Scotia, told me we are eating too high on the hog — or at least too high on the ecological pyramid of the sea. Conversion of sun energy and ocean minerals is an enormously wasteful process by every creature but the basic plant at the bottom of the pyramid. Passing the energy and minerals from microscopic water plants through the animals which graze on them, and the small fish that prey on them, and the big fish like the predatory cod that eat the little fish, requires 10,000 pounds at the bottom of the pyramid to put one pound of weight on a man.

"Eating so high on the pyramid is like feeding corn to chickens and feeding the chickens to rats and feeding the rats to cats and selling cat filet mignon in the supermarket. The process wastes good corn and chickens.

"We are going to have to adjust our eating habits to hard times coming. During the next 35 years we are going to have to increase the catch four to six times. Till now we've been regulating mesh size to let the little ones escape. The Chinese and Japanese fishing the East China Sea use as small a mesh as they can manage and catch *everything*. Every scrap of meat goes into the hopper. They catch four to six times as much per acre as our highly selective banks fishermen.

"The high seas belong to everybody. Wait till the Chinese show up on the banks. To feed that vast population they will have no choice but to sweep the banks clean of what we call marketable fish, leaving virtually nothing but fingerlings, grinding up everything for protein not for dollars. It is regrettable for the seafood gourmet, perhaps; but other fishermen will have no choice but to switch to the Chinese style of fishing because only tiny fish will survive.

"When you fish an area that hard, you work a big change in the size and species caught. On our banks the capelin and herring would flourish as the cod disappeared, but even they would become smaller. When they become too small for hu-

89

man consumption directly, you feed them as meal to chickens that, incidentally, are enormously efficient converters of protein. Eventually the fillet and steak would vanish but the total catch of protein would zoom.

"For example, the herring stocks of the Bay of Fundy are so vast nobody has ever measured them. They have been fished so hard they have shrunk and are sold as sardines. But the catch of sardines is bigger than the catch of mature fish ever was. The big factory ships from the hungry Old World countries probably have doomed the colorful small-time fisherman hunting the big cod, haddock, and halibut and other elite fish."

But H. R. Bradley of the Canadian fisheries enforcement division, whose job it is to guard the inshore fisheries against foreign poaching, has a different theory.

"You cannot fish out an area biologically in the sense that you wipe out a species. But you can fish it till it's not worth the trouble to go back.

"By law no foreigner can land his catch in Newfoundland or fish within 12 miles of our shoreline. He can come in for repairs, water, refueling, hospital service, reprovisioning, iceing, but he cannot unload his ship — except for the occasional American in trouble who has special treaty permission to land his catch to keep it from spoiling. That round trip here and back with each load of fish places a heavy economic strain on the foreign trawlers.

"This island lies right on top of the banks. When the big boys in the factory fleets suck up all the fish and decide they are not catching enough to pay for the expensive machinery, elaborate organization, and, above all, the expensive trip here and back, we'll still be fishing from this permanently anchored factory ship.

"Don't give up on the Newfoundlander. He's a tough old bird, and he'll survive and fish his own banks again when the industrial wonders have long since run home."

With a grim feeling that I may be whistling in the dark, I am betting on Mr. Bradley against Dr. Dickie. I should hate in my lifetime to see that sturdy island race and the hardy trawlermen become robots in a seagoing assembly line and forget how to ride out a storm in a dory, chop ice from the rigging, mend a net with bare hands in a blizzard. Or forget the chanteys their old grandfathers taught them to soften a hard but a virile life, a life that made iron men.

# Acknowledgments

The author and photographer wish to thank the following for their invaluable help:

Foremost is Newfoundland's Premier Joey Smallwood, who generously made the provincial fisheries training vessel available to us for cruises on the fisheries banks and also permitted free run of his splendid library of Newfoundlandiana.

Also helpful were: Russell Riley, consul-general of the United States then stationed in St. John's; Cecil Garland, local fisherman; Larry Gushue, general manager of the St. John's Tourist and Convention Bureau; Cyril Banikhin, of the provincial college of fisheries; Dr. Wilfred Templeman, of the Fisheries Research Board of Canada; Harry Stamp, of Publicity Services; the captains and crews of the *Atlantic Jane,* the *Atlantic Peggy,* and the *Beinir;* L. R. Day, Director of ICNAF; Dr. Lloyd Dickie, of the Bedford Institute of Oceanography; H. R. Bradley, of the enforcement division of the Department of Fisheries; Roland de Grosbois, of the Canadian Government Travel Bureau; and Miss Janet Thompson, of the Tourist and Convention Bureau.

The author is grateful to Yale University Press for permission to reprint the passage from *The Vinland Map and The Tartar Relation,* by R. A. Skelton, T. E. Marston, and G. D. Painter.

Verse from song "Squid Jiggin' Ground," reprinted with permission of BMI Canada Limited. Copyright 1944 by A. R. Scammel. Copyright assigned to BMI Canada Limited.

# Sources

Banks, Sir Joseph. *Journal of a Voyage to Newfoundland and Labrador Commencing April 7th and Ending November the 17th, 1766.*

Biddle, Richard. *A Memoir of Sebastian Cabot; with a Review of the History of Maritime Discovery.* London, 1831.

Brazão, Eduardo. *La Découverte de Terre-Neuve.* Montreal University Press, 1964.

Brown, Alexander C. *Women and Children Last.* New York, Putnam, 1961.

Doyle, G. S. *Old-Time Songs and Poetry of Newfoundland.* Gerald S. Doyle Limited, St. John's, Newfoundland.

English, L. E. F. *Historic Newfoundland.* St. John's, Newfoundland, 1965.

Gaudia, E. de "Primitivos Navegantes Vascos." *Revista Interior de los Estudios Vascos.* San Sebastian, Tome XV, No. 1.

Hakluyt, Richard. *Principal Navigations, voiages and discoveries of the English nation.* Cambridge University Press, 1965. 2 vols.

Innis, Harold Adams. *The Cod Fisheries.* Toronto, University of Toronto Press, 1954.

Lacy, B. *Miscellaneous Poems Compos'd at Newfoundland, on Board His Majesty's ship the Kinsale.* London, 1729.

Larson, Lawrence M. "Did John Scolous Visit Labrador and Newfoundland in or about 1476?" *Scandinavian Studies.* May, 1922.

Lounsbury, Ralph Greenlee. *The British Fishery at Newfoundland 1634-1763.* Yale University Press, 1934.

Mills, Alan, and Peacock, Kenneth. *Favourite Songs of Newfoundland.* BMI Canada Ltd., Toronto.

Morandière, Charles de la. *Histoire de la Pêche Francaise de la Morue dans l'Amérique Septentrionale.* G. P. Maisonneuve et Larose, Paris, 1962.

Oleson, Tryggvi Julius. *Early Voyages and Northern Approaches, 1000-1632.* McClelland, Toronto, 1963.

Oxenstierna, Eric. "The Vikings," *Scientific American.* May, 1967, Vol. 216, pp. 67-78.

Payne, Edward John, and Beazley, C. R. *Voyages of Elizabethan Seamen Selected from "Principal Navigations" by Hakluyt.* London, 1907.

Prowse, Daniel W. *A History of Newfoundland* from the English, colonial and foreign records. London, Macmillan, 1895.

Ronciere, Charles de la. *Le Premier Routier Pilote de Terre Neuve.* Chartres, 1904.

Skelton, R. A., Marston, T. E., and Painter, G. D. *The Vinland Map and The Tartar Relation.* Yale University Press, 1965.

Templeman, Wilfred. *Marine Resources of Newfoundland.* Fisheries Research Board of Canada, Ottawa, 1966.

Villiers, Alan. *The Quest of the Schooner Argus; a voyage to the Banks and Greenland.* New York, Scribners, 1949.

Winters, G. H. *The Capelin, Newfoundland's Latent Resource.* Fisheries Research Board. St. John's, Newfoundland.

Annual Proceedings, Vol. 16. International Commission for the Northwest Atlantic Fisheries. Dartmouth, Nova Scotia, 1966.

*Chafe's Sealing Book, 1863-1938.* Trade Printers, St. John's, Newfoundland.

Environmental Symposium, International Commission for the Northwest Atlantic Fisheries. Dartmouth, Nova Scotia, 1965.

Fourth Annual Report, 1965. Bedford Institute of Oceanography. Dartmouth, Nova Scotia.

ICNAF Newsletter, No. 44. Bedford Institute of Oceanography. Dartmouth, Nova Scotia.

*Log Book, HMS Pegasus, 1786.* (Under command of HRH Prince William Henry, later William IV.)

"To the Printer," letter to *The London Chronicle.* September 16, 1762.

The World Food Problem, A Report of the President's Science Advisory Committee, Vols. I and II, 1967.

Printed in U.S.A.